AMERICAN BATTLEFIELD OF A
EUROPEAN WAR

THE FRENCH AND INDIAN WAR

US History Elementary

Children's American Revolution History

BABY PROFESSOR

EDUCATION KIDS

Speedy Publishing LLC

40 E. Main St. #1156

Newark, DE 19711

www.speedypublishing.com

Copyright 2017

THE FRENCH AND INDIAN WAR

France and England fought wars against each other for almost a thousand years. They weren't fighting all the time, but the next war was never far away.

The French and Indian War was one part of the long struggle between these two European powers, though this part took place in North America. Read on and learn more about this war!

A Battle of the French-Indian War

Conference Between the French and Native American Leaders

A WAR WITH A CONFUSING NAME

The French and Indian War is a part of the Seven Years' War which took place from 1756 to 1763. The Seven Years' War was a conflict all around the world between France and Great Britain. Some people call it the first world war!

The French and Indian war was the part of this conflict that took place in North America, as both European countries tried to extend their power and territory. Spain also wanted to expand its control of the New World, and played a small part in the war.

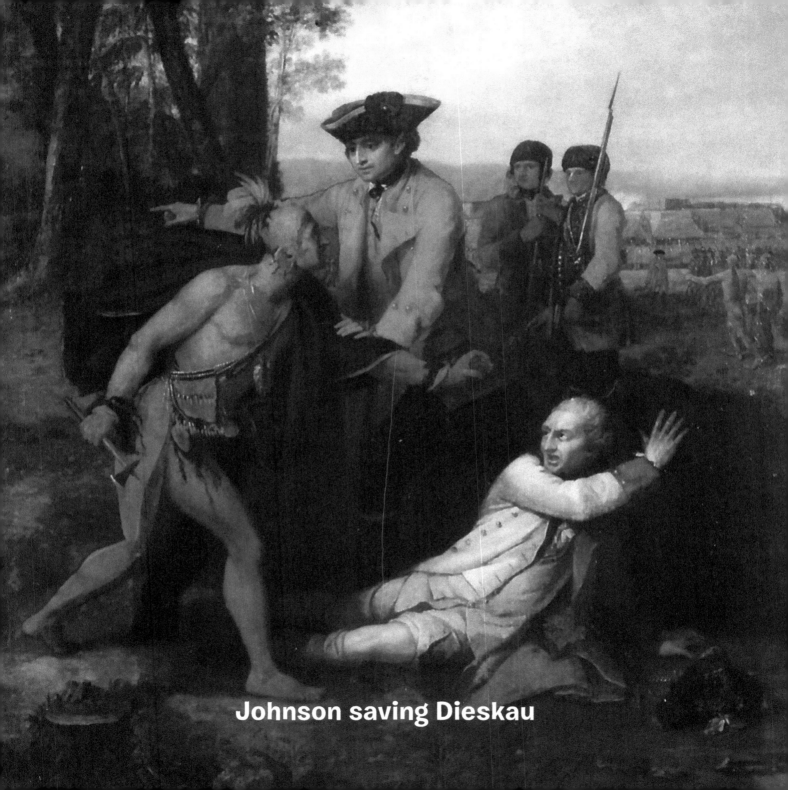

Johnson saving Dieskau

Great Britain had colonies all along the east coast of North America, while France controlled what is now Quebec, areas around the Great Lakes, and part of Nova Scotia. Spain held what is now Florida and Cuba.

WHERE ARE THE INDIANS?

"Indians" is in the name of the war, but Native Americans were not just on one side. Some tribes supported the French, and some tribes worked with the English.

Creek War Treaty

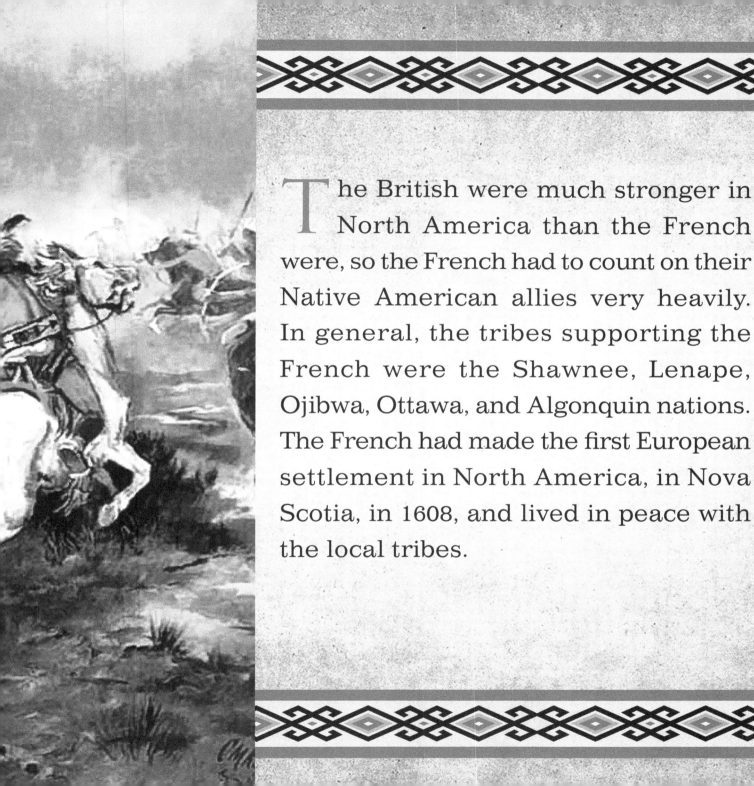

The British were much stronger in North America than the French were, so the French had to count on their Native American allies very heavily. In general, the tribes supporting the French were the Shawnee, Lenape, Ojibwa, Ottawa, and Algonquin nations. The French had made the first European settlement in North America, in Nova Scotia, in 1608, and lived in peace with the local tribes.

In general, French colonists worked more peacefully with Native Americans they met, tried to learn their languages and often adopted elements of their culture. They learned many ways of fighting from the Native Americans that were more suited for war in heavily-wooded land. This put the British armies, which liked to wear bright uniforms and march in careful ranks, at a disadvantage.

Soldiers firing guns in the Battle of Waterloo

Cherokee Indians

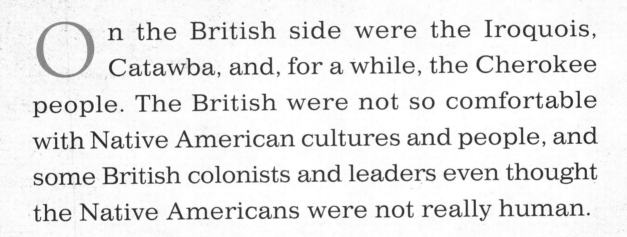

On the British side were the Iroquois, Catawba, and, for a while, the Cherokee people. The British were not so comfortable with Native American cultures and people, and some British colonists and leaders even thought the Native Americans were not really human.

As the war went on, the tribes had a hard time deciding, not only which side would win, but what outcome in this war of two invaders would be best for the people who had been in the land for tens of thousands of years.

French Indian War

French Troops

AT FIRST, THE FRENCH WIN

As French traders and colonists expanded from Quebec south across the Great Lakes and into what is now Ohio, they came into conflict with English colonists and settlers expanding west from New York, Pennsylvania, and Virginia. In 1754 these conflicts exploded into war.

In 1754 and 1755 the French won a series of battles in the west. The British began to be afraid that French settlers in Nova Scotia would rise up in revolt, so they rounded up the "Acadians" and deported most of them from Nova Scotia to places like Louisiana.

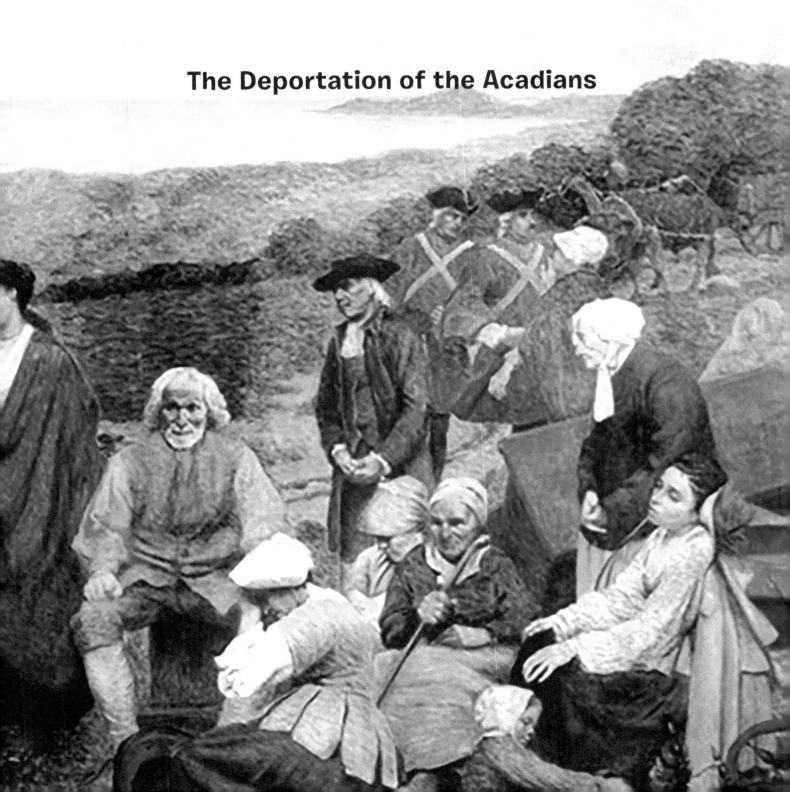

The Deportation of the Acadians

French troops waving flags for victory

Great Britain's leaders paid little attention to the war in the colonies at first, and did not send much in the way of extra troops or supplies. The British assumed that their armies could defeat any French army, and it took a stunning series of losses to change their minds.

The French captured Fort Oswego in 1756, taking over a thousand prisoners. When they captured Fort William Henry in 1757, the French and their Native American allies made terms of surrender with the British to end the battle. Then they broke the terms once the British came out of the fort, and killed over 150 British soldiers.

Stone Castle of Fort William Henry

William Pitt

THE ENGLISH STRIKE BACK

In 1757 the new leader of the British government, William Pitt, decided that winning the war with the French could give Great Britain an empire that would reach almost around the world. He borrowed great amounts of money to pay for supplies and hire troops to fight in the colonies.

Fortress of Louisbourg

In 1758 the British attacked and captured the Fortress of Louisbourg in Cape Breton, now part of Nova Scotia. This was France's strongest point on the Atlantic coast, and capturing it opened the way for British ships to sail up the Saint Lawrence River to bring the war to Quebec. A month after capturing Louisbourg in the east, the British captured Fort Frontenac at the western end of the Saint Lawrence.

City of Quebec

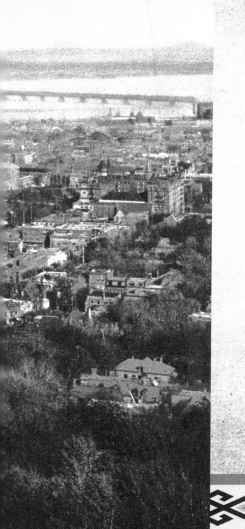

Then, in 1759, the British attacked the city and fortress of Quebec. It took a long while, and a dangerous climb up cliffs, to get the army into position. Then, when the two armies met, the battle was over in one hour with a huge British victory.

The British followed up this victory by capturing Montreal, the last major French settlement, in 1760. With French Canada now in British hands, Great Britain moved to attacking French and Spanish territory all around the world, as Spain had become an ally of France.

Capturing Montreal

Mississippi River Valley

THE RESULTS OF THE WAR

The war formally ended with a peace conference in 1763. Great Britain gained all of French North America from France and gained Florida from Spain. This made Great Britain's colonies stronger and more secure, and made it possible for English settlers to move into the Mississippi River valley and further west. Great Britain was well on the way to building a global empire.

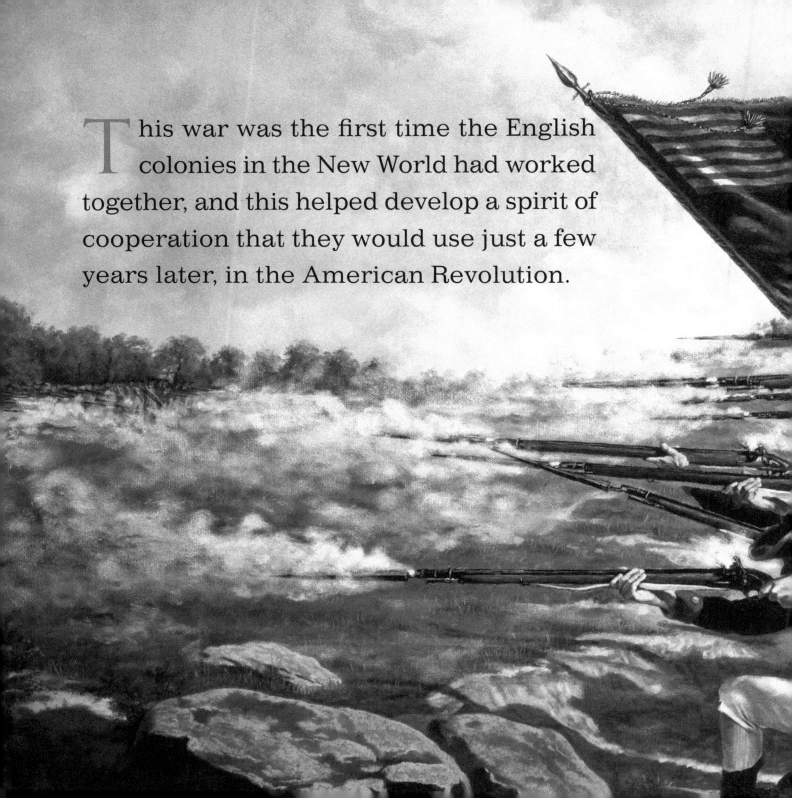

This war was the first time the English colonies in the New World had worked together, and this helped develop a spirit of cooperation that they would use just a few years later, in the American Revolution.

American Revolution

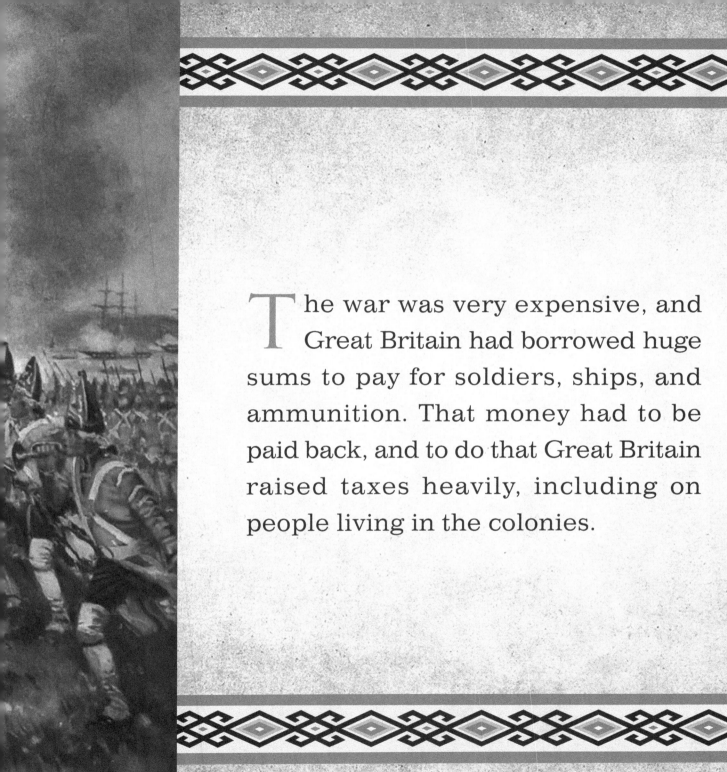

The war was very expensive, and Great Britain had borrowed huge sums to pay for soldiers, ships, and ammunition. That money had to be paid back, and to do that Great Britain raised taxes heavily, including on people living in the colonies.

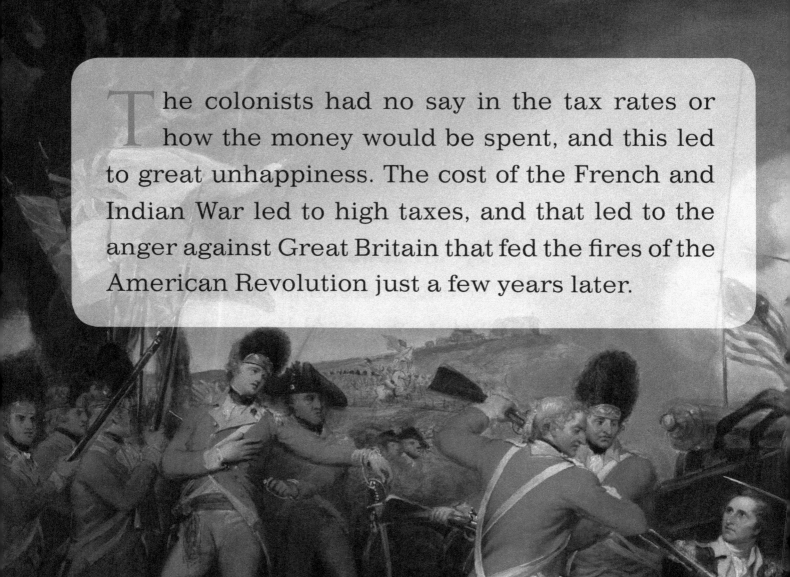

The colonists had no say in the tax rates or how the money would be spent, and this led to great unhappiness. The cost of the French and Indian War led to high taxes, and that led to the anger against Great Britain that fed the fires of the American Revolution just a few years later.

American Revolution

Daniel Boone

INTERESTING FACTS ABOUT THE WAR

Here are some fun facts about this oddly-named war.

- Daniel Boone, a famous woodsman, was the driver of a supply wagon for the army during this war.

- George Washington, later a great general in the American Revolution and the first President of the United States, was a twenty-three-year-old colonel. He fought (and lost) the very first battle of the war.

- The British captured part of Cuba from Spain in 1762 during the war. They traded their gains back to Spain in return for Florida at the end of the war.

- Louisiana has a distinct culture of French-speaking "Cajuns". The Cajuns are the descendants of the Acadians who were expelled from Nova Scotia in the 1760s.

Acadians

Native American Warrrior

Both French and British forces learned guerrilla-warfare tactics from the Native Americans: dressing in camouflage, moving silently through the woods, and setting ambushes for their enemy. As a song of the time complained, "They fought so unfairly from back of the trees! If they'd only fought open we'd have beat 'em with ease."

In 1749, the French started posting lead plaques along the Ohio River valley to claim the territory for France. The hope was that English settlers would respect the claim and not move further west. The settlers basically ignored the plaques!

Ohio River Valley

French Troops

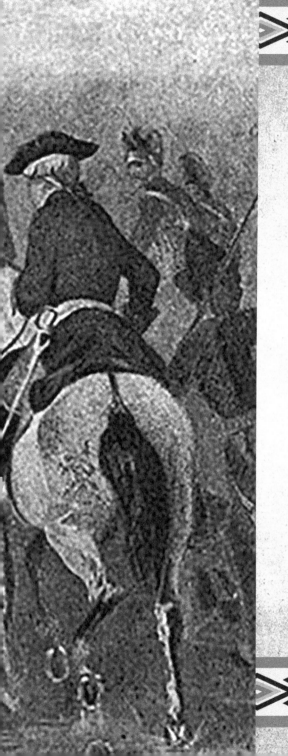

Sometimes the people fighting in this war were very polite. When the British were getting ready to assault Louisbourg, the British general sent two pineapples to the wife of the French commander, with an apology for any inconvenience she might experience. The French commander's wife sent back a letter of thanks, and some bottles of champagne.

In Western movies, often the scary Native Americans are shown scalping their victims. The British taught this practice to their Native American allies: they would pay a certain amount of money for each scalp that a warrior brought to the fort to prove how many people he had killed. Before this, scalping was not a Native American habit.

Native American Tribe

In 1758 a British force of 15,000 soldiers sailed up Lake George in what is now New York to attack the French Fort Carillon on Lake Champlain. There were fewer than four thousand French soldiers, but they were able to build defenses of sharpened tree branches and pits. The defenses slowed down the British advance so the French riflemen could shoot them without being shot at. The British attack failed.

Lake George

LONG-TIME ENEMIES AND ALLIES

⚜

France and England have been both friends and enemies since the time of the Roman Empire. For most of the past thousand years the two countries were rivals, though since 1900 they have been allies and colleagues. Read about one of their great conflicts, before the time of the French and Indian War, in the Baby Professor book Royals Hold Grudges for One Hundred Years!

Visit

BABY PROFESSOR
EDUCATION KIDS

www.BabyProfessorBooks.com

to download Free Baby Professor eBooks
and view our catalog of new and exciting
Children's Books